PASSPORT
TO THE
LAND OF
ENOUGH

Joel Nagel

Passport to the Land of Enough

©2015 by Joel Nagel

ISBN: 978-1-939086-96-9

Illumination Publishers is committed to caring wisely for God's creation and uses recycled paper whenever possible. Printed in the United States.

Cover design by Neville McKinnie and Interior layout by Joel Nagel.

About the author: Joel Nagel has led the Lansing Area Church of Christ in Lansing, Michigan since 2002. He studied history at Michigan State University where he focused on building a campus ministry. When not advancing the gospel or spending time with his family, Joel loves trail running and exploring waterfalls in Michigan's Upper Peninsula. He and his wife, Beth, have two daughters.

www.ipibooks.com
6010 Pinecreek Ridge Court
Spring, Texas 77379-2513

Foreword

I'm reminded very consistently that I'm the "oldest guy," ministry wise, on the staff of the Chicago Church of Christ. Baptized in 1976 at the Crossroads Church in Gainesville, Florida, I've been around for almost four decades, serving as a minister for nearly 35 years. In that time, I've heard or delivered hundreds of lessons on giving and participated in countless missions contributions. I have been personally inspired by others many times, and prayerfully have been able to inspire generosity in groups I've had the privilege to serve.

But in all that time, I cannot remember being challenged or convicted the way I was when I read Joel Nagel's *Passport to the Land of Enough.* I first perused this guide early in 2014 and began to work through the materials, visit the websites, accept the challenges and examine my own heart. I decided quickly that this information needed to be delivered to the ministry that I led at the time. It has had a profound impact on everyone who has taken seriously the teaching and challenges it contains.

In the Parable of the Sower, Jesus warns that many who hear the Word will be choked by "life's worries, riches and pleasures." We who live in the First World countries are among the wealthiest people in the world and are barraged daily by the world's unending messages: "Make more money! Buy more things! Build bigger houses! Drive nicer cars! Buy recreational toys! And shoes! You need more shoes! You can't afford this? No worries—we have a credit card for you! What's in your wallet?"

Joel's penetrating words are a clarion call to stop, examine ourselves and make changes—dramatic changes—in the lifestyle decisions we make on a daily basis: the way that we view wealth, the way that we live and the way that we share the resources that God so graciously pours out on us.

As a powerful voice from a new generation of evangelists, Joel has written for us a courageous challenge to the status quo, a vigorous call to disciples all over the world who live in a land of plenty to move—on a heart level—to the land of enough.

—Dave Eastman
Evangelist, Chicago Church of Christ

PASSPORT INFORMATION

NAME

CHURCH

MISSIONS DESTINATION

ACCOUNTABILITY PARTNER

PASSPORT AGREEMENT

I, the undersigned, agree with the following:

As a member of God's kingdom I am blessed beyond what I can fathom both here and in the life to come. I may not be able to experience life as a disciple in another country but I recognize that there is great suffering going on among "the family of believers throughout the world." I am in a unique position to use my resources to help my brothers and sisters who are fellow citizens with me in God's kingdom.

I therefore pledge to use this passport to travel to a missions destination that will allow my resources to be used for God's glory. That destination is the **"Land of Enough."**

As a bearer of this passport I agree to honestly examine my heart in the light of God's word and make every effort to make it to a place where I am content with what I have and able to be the "cheerful giver" that God loves.

I pledge to be honest and courageous as I give my whole heart to this month-long journey of faith.

Signature _____ Date _____

For maximum impact, choose an accountability partner that you will meet with throughout the month.

Partner Signature _____

PASSPORT OVERVIEW

"Two things I ask of you, Lord; do not refuse me before I die: Keep falsehood and lies far from me; give me neither poverty nor riches, but give me only my daily bread. Otherwise, I may have too much and disown you and say, 'Who is the Lord?' Or I may become poor and steal, and so dishonor the name of my God."

—Proverbs 30:7-9

I'm sure that God hears millions of prayers for riches every day, but how often does he hear something like the remarkable prayer of Agur? Agur prays for "neither poverty nor riches." He prays to just have **enough**. This is already challenging! It's as if "enough" is a faraway place that we would love to visit but we have no idea how to get there.

The goal of this passport is to use the Scriptures as our GPS on an epic journey from our cities and towns to the **Land of Enough.** We will also experience what it is like to be a disciple of Christ in other countries. No plane tickets are necessary, yet we will end up in a very different place than where we started.

MAKING A DIFFERENCE

Let's do more than just read about the physically and spiritually poor around the world. Let's change the world as we change ourselves. Many will experience this adventure while participating in one of the hallmarks of our fellowship of churches: our yearly special missions contribution. If our hearts can become content with enough, then our brothers and sisters around the world will be blessed with the "more than enough" that we may be holding on to. If you are taking this journey outside of your church's special missions collection, begin thinking now about who you can help along the way.

You can learn more about our fellowship of churches and special missions at:

www.disciplestoday.com

WEEKLY

Each week we will land on a new theme and meet people from churches all over the world. If you are reading this as part of a churchwide campaign, there is space for you to write notes from the sermons you'll hear. Otherwise you can just use the space to reflect and take notes at the end of each week.

Families should be sure to participate in the **Family Night Devotional** that corresponds with each week's theme. Be sure to try the **Recipe of the Week** to truly get a taste of what it would be like to be a disciple in another part of the world.

DAILY

Start each day by reading the scriptures and devotional. Take thorough travel notes in the space provided. Visiting the daily **Web Links** will greatly enhance this adventure, even from the comfort of your smartphone or web browser.

Each day, there is a **Mission Challenge** that corresponds with the devotional. Many of the challenges will take some forethought. You can look over all of the mission challenges at the start of each week and begin planning ahead for the activities that interest you. The challenges are what make this journey interactive by helping you relate to your brothers and sisters around the world. Many will also help you save money that can be used to help those who have less.

Individuals and families who visit the daily web links and take the mission challenges will get so much more impact from these lessons. To access the links on your smartphone, download a **QR code** reader like "Red Laser" from the App Store or Google Play.

CHURCH WIDE

Your entire church can participate in the Passport To Land Of Enough. If you are a ministry leader you can head over to **www.landofenough.com** and click on the **Ministry Leaders** tab to get free access to sermon outlines, campaign resources and ideas that will inspire your whole congregation.

CELEBRATION

MISSION

BOUNDARIES

PERSPECTIVE

CONVICTION

WEEK ONE

PERSPECTIVE

PERSPECTIVE

"There was a rich man who would dress in purple and fine linen, feasting lavishly every day. But a poor man named Lazarus, covered with sores, was left at his gate."

—Luke 16:19-20 (HCSB)

This is going to hurt. But the intention is not to make you feel bad. Before we can move to the Land of Enough, we have to figure out where we currently stand. Are we the nameless rich man or are we the poor and sick Lazarus? Or, as is more likely the case, do we stand somewhere between the gate and the banquet table?

We need to look at the numbers and assess our wealth. But, we can't just look at the numbers. We have to let the numbers sink in. The amount of money, food or time we have are merely numbers. How those things affect our hearts is what counts. Many people rush through life and give little thought to what they make and have and do. In this first week we will hit the pause button and take an intimate look at the quantifiable parts of our lives. This will take time and effort, but it's worth it!

Here's the painful part: We'll also look at how our wealth compares to the world's poorest people. The world's poor represent almost half of all the people alive today. They (3 billion people) live on $2.50 a day or less. You may have never met one of them but they probably sewed the shirt you're wearing and made your child's favorite toy. In order to truly understand how much we have, we need to compare ourselves with those who have so little. There is nothing inherently wrong with being rich or poor. It's our heart toward wealth or poverty that gets us into trouble. This week we will just look at the cold hard facts and get our minds and hearts thinking. Next week we'll let God's word tell us what to do with what we discover.

First let's imagine what it would be like if you or your family were disciples in one of the poor churches we support with our special missions contribution.

IF YOU LIVED IN INDIA...

How would your life be different if you lived in India? Maybe it would be like that of Vency Babitha. Her family of 5 live in a village near Trivandrum, on the southwest tip of India. There are palm trees and fresh fruits. Nearby, you can see the sunrise and sunset from the same outcropping of rocks on the Indian Ocean. It would be a paradise if they weren't so poor. Vency is the youngest of three children who live in a small hut in a traditional Indian village.

Vency's father is a farmer by trade but his work is sporadic. Her older brother works in a factory and her older sister works at the hospital. Vency works 9 hours a day as a maid bringing in $40 for the family each month (or what we may make in half a day). All together, the family earns just under $10 per day, putting them below the world poverty marker of $2.50 per person per day.

We can easily react with judgment or assumptions about the poor. This family is not poor because they are lazy. On the contrary, they work very hard and they do it while sometimes skipping meals and suffering through constant heat. Also, we should not assume they are poor money managers. Many Americans get by just fine without really tracking their finances. But even though Vency's family has so little, they must go to great lengths to plan ahead and take care of their money. The world's poor lack access to financial institutions so their money is hidden, safeguarded by relatives and even loaned to those who have less than them. They cannot live day to day because their sources of income bring little security. Even with so little, they have responsibly saved money and goods for the lean times and emergencies.

Although poor, they are not defined by their poverty. They are your brothers and sisters in Christ and they find their true identity in him.

MISSION CHALLENGES

This week's mission challenges are designed to help you gain perspective. It's one thing to read about the world's poor; it's a whole other thing to experience little pieces of their lives. Look over this list and decide which challenges you and your family may want to take on this week. It's okay if you need to do a challenge on a different day. The important thing is trying!

Day 1
Limit your spending on food to $2.50 for the entire day. Some of our brothers and sisters only have that much for *all* of their expenses but for this challenge we will just limit our food budget.

Day 2
Spend an evening at home with your family in only one room of your house. Eat, play and sleep together in that small space. See this week's Family Devotional for helpful activities.

Day 3
Leave the car in the driveway and take public transportation, carpool or foot power to a church event sometime this month. While you're at it, share your faith along the way!

Day 4
Fast from a luxury item for the rest of the month. Apply the money you save to your special missions contribution or charity. Can you say no to coffee?

Day 5
Clear your cupboards! Decide not to go grocery shopping until you've actually eaten all of the food in your cupboards—yes, even that can of artichoke hearts!

Day 6
In the Old Testament, going to worship always included bringing gifts to the temple. Look through your possessions. Give someone a thoughtful gift at the next church service.

FAMILY NIGHT DEVOTIONAL

Sing Have each child choose a song.

Opener Have each family member go get their favorite toy/possession. Talk about why they like it. How would they feel if it was gone?

Scripture Matthew 6:25-34

Discuss Have a brief, age appropriate talk. What are some ways that our family is rich? In what ways do you worry about your wealth and possessions? What do you wish we had? What does it look like to seek his kingdom and righteousness first?

Activity Spend the rest of the night in one room in your house. Eat and sleep there on the floor. Play games and talk. Imagine what it would have been like to live in the times of Jesus. Talk to your children about the most important things: God and family.

Game Play board games together in your one room.

Pray!

RECIPE OF THE WEEK

This week's recipe was suggested by a disciple who lives on the very southernmost tip of india in Kanyakumari. **Palotta** is a flat bread recipe that will be fun for the whole family to make together. The ingredients are common and inexpensive. You can use a griddle or even a frying pan. Scan the QR code or type in the link to get the recipe.

Ingredients
1 cup whole wheat flour
1 cup all purpose flour
2 Tbsps oil
¼ tsp baking soda
¾ to 1 cup hot water
1 to 2 tsp sugar
¾ tsp salt or as required

landofenough.com/recipes

DAY 1:
WEALTH

How much do I have?

How much do my brothers and sisters have?

SCRIPTURE

Luke 12:13-21

"I will tear down my barns and build bigger ones."

MISSION CHALLENGE

Limit your spending on food to $2.50 for an entire day. Some of our brothers and sisters only have that much for *all* of their expenses but for this challenge we will just limit our food budget. It will be hard, but try your best.

AM I RICH?

In our hearts, we know that "life does not consist in an abundance of possessions." But our thoughts and actions often tell a different story. Whether you see yourself as someone with a little or a lot, the thought process of the rich fool closely parallels the common American dream. We want our wealth, position, possessions and bank accounts to grow. To be content with what you have is almost un-American. Besides, it's not like we are rich!

That's where we need perspective. Vency and her family are among the world's truly poor. Their income is below the world poverty marker of $2.50 per person per day. They are not poor because of laziness. They work long hours at tough jobs. They are poor because they were born where 1 in 7 people are born: India.

It is easy for us to read passages like this and think, "What a rich fool!" But we might just be condemning ourselves if we don't have perspective about how truly wealthy even some of the poorest Americans are. The information you write on the next page will form an important foundation for the rest of this book. Don't skip it! Take time now to reflect and write. There is more space at the back of the book for extra notes if you need it.

REFLECT AND WRITE

How much money do you (or your family) make in a year?

How much per month?

How much each day?

How do you honestly feel about the money that you make?

Can you imagine living on $2.50 per day?

What kind of housing could you afford?

What would your food consist of?

What would you do if you got sick or hurt?

These are questions that most of us don't have to answer, but that almost half of the world wrestles with every day.

Put yourself in the Vency's shoes: What would she think of your lifestyle? How would she spend your money?

ACT

Don't take your wealth for granted. If you are not on a budget you won't be able to make wise decisions about your wealth. Track your spending for the next 7 days; **www.mint.com** is a great free resource.

Web Link
You'll be surprised by how wealthy you really are! This is a must-see:

Snap the QR code with your smart phone or visit www.landofenough.com

DAY 2:
BASICS

How much do
I have to worry
about?

What if I had
less?

SCRIPTURE

Matthew 6:25-26

"Do not worry about
your life..."

MISSION CHALLENGE

Spend an evening at
home with your family
in only one room of your
house (a smaller room).
Eat, play and sleep to-
gether in that small
space. See this week's
Family Devotional for
helpful activities.

FOOD, SHELTER, CLOTHING

From their less than $2.50 per day, Vency's fam-
ily must supply food, clothing and shelter. Their
food consists mostly of rice. Sometimes they
can afford beans and occasionally fish. Most of
the time, because of frugality and good money
management, they eat three meals per day despite their poverty. But in hard times they may
skip a meal or only eat one meal per day.

Poor people like Vency have only a couple of
sets of clothing that get washed once per week
by hand. Even this small amount of laundry takes
hours of hard scrubbing.

They live in a village hut-house. Huts often lack
bathrooms, electricity and running water. They
are designed for airflow because of the constant
heat.

As disciples, their family faces the same
temptation to worry as we do, but in a very
different way. When they worry about the basics
it is truly because their lives may be threatened.
Yet, Jesus' words still ring true and worrying will
not add anything to their lives either. How will
this perspective change the way you view your
possessions?

REFLECT AND WRITE

How much do you spend weekly on groceries and eating out?

How long could you go without wearing the same outfit twice?

How much do you pay per month for housing (rent, mortgage, utilities)?

480,00

How different would your life be if you were malnourished and hungry most of the time? How would your dreams and ambitions change? If you have children, think about how different their childhoods would be.

Not everything about having less is negative. How much more simple would your life be if you had less clothing and less space to clean and maintain?

What would be different about your family if you all lived in the same room? How would your relationships with your neighbors change if you shared a kitchen and bathroom?

ACT

Skip a meal this week and pray about the world's poor every time you feel hungry.

> **Web Link**
> How does your weekly grocery bill compare with families around the world?
>
> Snap the QR code with your smartphone or visit www.landofenough.com

TIME

How much time do I really have?

What if I was less busy and more productive?

SCRIPTURE

Ecclesiastes 3:1

"There is a time for everything..."

MISSION CHALLENGE

Leave the car in the driveway and take public transportation, carpool or foot power to a church event sometime this month. While you're at it, share your faith along the way!

TIME IS MONEY

In our society, modern conveniences give us a lot of extra time when we compare our schedules to that of the world's poor. Washing machines and dryers do work that takes hours of intense labor. When we want to go somewhere many of us just hop in our cars while our third world brothers and sisters wait for unreliable and sparse public transportation or just walk. The world's poor spend hours cooking the little food that they have. They go to bed exhausted from days full of hard labor. They have little leisure time and the idea of "me time" which is touted as essential for Americans is a fleeting thought.

Vency and her family are busy with things that keep them alive. They work long hours. To attend church they must use unreliable public buses and they often end up walking the 12 miles from their village to the church. Even though they are exhausted, they make time and go to great lengths to encourage their brothers and sisters in the Trivandrum church. Vency arrives early to decorate. She is eager to make disciples in her village that is filled with idolatry. Disciples in India will miss a weekend of work (and pay) to attend conferences to learn how to be Bible talk leaders. Special missions contribution helps pay for the train fare to bring them across India.

When they are not working they are resting or doing kingdom work. They do not have "me time" or even privacy like we have. India is the same size as the continental United States but has 3 times the population. Almost everything they do takes more time and is more difficult for them than it would be for us. Yet, they rarely complain.

REFLECT AND WRITE

Do you frequently feel stressed?

Do you have a good grasp on how you spend your time?

If you treated time like money, would you be "time rich" by the world's standards? How well do you manage the often overlooked asset of time? As a disciple of Christ, does your schedule reflect self-denial for the kingdom of God?

How would your life be different without some of the modern conveniences that save us time? How would your relationships change if you could only talk to people face to face after traveling to see them? How much more would you share your faith if you took public transportation everywhere you went?

ACT

Write out your schedule and create a "time budget." Set limits or goals for how much time you will spend on things like watching TV and playing with the kids. Prioritize the things that matter most to you. Look at your schedule and take control of your (God's) time.

Web Link
Speaking of time: What was the best time in history to be born?

Snap the QR code with your smartphone or visit www.landofenough.com

DAY 4:
LUXURY

How luxurious is my life?

By what standard should I measure my wealth?

SCRIPTURE

James 5:5

"You have lived on earth in luxury..."

MISSION CHALLENGE

Fast from a luxury item for the rest of the month. Apply the money you save to your special missions contribution or a charity. Can you say no to coffee?

EXAMINING THE EXTRAS

Many of the things that we consider normal parts of everyday life would be luxuries in Vency's family. In India, if you want to send your children to school you have to pay. Thus, many of the poor are uneducated or partly educated. Even though they all work, they do not own a car. It is not uncommon to see a family of 5 on a moped in India. But Vency is too poor even for that. They do not have money to waste on caffeine or entertainment. A church retreat would be the closest thing to a vacation they would ever have. But even then they would have to sacrifice income to attend.

They are poor but surviving. Yet, one injury or illness could quickly change that. The world's poor often do not have access to health care outside of aid clinics run by nonprofits. Although they are vital, these clinics require long waits for even the most basic care. If one member of the family is unable to work, their level of poverty quickly becomes life threatening.

The family, however, is not without luxury. They cherish their Bibles and they have a great network of relations through church. So they have the greatest luxuries, just not the same things we immediately associate with luxury.

REFLECT AND WRITE

Record the amount you spend on the following luxuries: caffeine, entertainment, fitness, healthcare, car, clothes, education and vacation.

Do the luxuries that you enjoy (some undoubtedly seem like necessities) bring you true joy and happiness? Do they bring glory to God? If you didn't have some of your luxuries, what would others think of you? In the time and money you saved by not indulging you could do more purposeful things for God. Can you think of some things that would bring God glory if they replaced your luxury?

Also consider this: some luxuries put us in self-defeating cycles. Like we eat too much so we need to go to the gym.

ACT

Pick one or two luxuries that you enjoy and fast from them for the rest of the month. A fast from something is different from just quitting it. When you fast, whenever you desire the thing you gave up, you can say a prayer and draw near to God. He is the only thing we truly need. Fasting from our luxuries can put that truth back into focus.

> **Web Link**
> *How does your spending compare with the average American?*
>
> *Snap the QR code with your smartphone or visit www.landofenough.com*

work harder on exercise

coffee - Buy

23

DAY 5:
DEBT

How much do I owe?

What does the Bible say about debt?

SCRIPTURE

Proverbs 6:1-8

"Free yourself, like a gazelle..."

MISSION CHALLENGE

Clear your cupboards! Decide not to go grocery shopping until you've actually eaten all of the food in your cupboards—yes, even that last can of artichoke hearts! This will help you relate more intimately with our Indian brothers.

SHACKLED

You might be surprised to know that people in the third world have debt. But it is of a different nature than most of ours. Poor people do not have access to financial institutions like banks and credit unions. So, they rely on each other when times get tough. At any one time Vency might owe her parents $20 while at the same time her neighbor owes her $5. Despite having so little, their money is always moving and shifting to take care of their needs as a family.

Families like Vency's also practice saving, but again, it is very different from our savings accounts and retirement plans. Indian women customarily keep one handful of rice back from each recipe and save it in a jar for lean times.

If they were poorer or disabled, they might have lost their children to kidnappers who take children off the streets and make them beg. Few of the beggars in India beg for themselves. Despite the corruption, the disciples in India always keep small coins to give to all who ask.

REFLECT AND WRITE

How much debt do you have? How much do you spend each month paying off debt? Do you have a plan to pay off your debts more quickly than just paying the minimum?

If you had no debt, how much money would you need to make to support your current lifestyle? Imagine the extra time and extra money that you could use to enrich others. But, the trap of the first world is to keep getting into debt and then working more to support a lifestyle beyond our means and then getting into more debt and making more money but never being able to use it for the good we desire deep down.

Another trap we fall into is to not give to God or to hold back from God while we focus on our debt. We work during church events. We give less than we should. What is God's desire for us in regard to debt?

ACT

Use the debt snowball method to get an idea of how you could pay off your debt. Talk to your accountability partner and come up with a plan. Run for your life from debt!

Web Link
Discover how quickly you can pay off all of your debt.

Snap the QR code with your smartphone or visit www.landofenough.com

25

DAY 6:
GIVING

How generous am I?

Would Jesus consider me a giving person?

SCRIPTURE

Malachi 3:10

Luke 21:1-4

"Jesus...saw the rich..."

MISSION CHALLENGE

Under the Old Covenant, going to worship always included giving gifts to the temple. Look through all your possessions and give someone a thoughtful gift at the next church service. Perhaps make it a quarterly practice, as it will help you know who is in need.

SACRIFICE

Poor people struggle with greed just like us. We think that rich people are obsessed with money; that is why they have so much. But poor people can be just as obsessed with what they don't have. Yet, Vency is not greedy despite her great poverty because she is a disciple of Jesus Christ.

If you were to visit her humble home, like any Christian's home in the third world, she would put an amazing spread before you with a giant smile on her face. (You would have to decline because our water sanitization systems make our bodies incompatible with anything cooked in an Indian home!)

To say that Vency tithes would be an understatement. Even the poorest strive to give 10% of their money but they also give in other ways. Indian disciples who have houses, house those in need. They cook meals for the sick. They pay bus fare for disciples who can't afford to get to church. When they hear about churches like ours giving special missions contribution each year they have mixed emotions. They are so joyful and grateful for their rich brothers and sisters. Yet, they also wish they didn't need such help. The churches in India get closer each year to being self-supporting.

REFLECT AND WRITE

How much do you give? Divide your yearly income by your yearly contribution. What percentage of your income do you give away? Would you like to give more? What is keeping you from giving more?

Imagine you had a million dollars to give away. What would you do with it? How would your money impact the needy? The church? People like Vency and her family?

The truth is, most of us will make well over a million dollars in our lifetime. Yet, we get tied down with payments, debts, luxuries and overspending. We want to give when the time is right. We tell ourselves that we are giving people, we just have bad finances. But for many, there will never be a perfect time to give. What if we stopped thinking about how much we have to give, but instead, measured our giving by the needs that need to be met?

ACT

If you are not tithing, take God at his word and start tithing right away (it will make next week's lessons easier to swallow).

Web Link
Take a trip to our sister churches in India and Asia.

Snap the QR code with your smartphone or visit www.landofenough.com

27

REST AND REFLECT

USE THIS SPACE TO REVIEW
THIS WEEK'S LESSONS AND
TAKE NOTES ON SUNDAY'S
SERMON.

WEEK TWO

CONVICTION

CONVICTION

"'Which of these three do you think was a neighbor to the man who fell into the hands of robbers?' The expert in the law replied, 'The one who had mercy on him.' Jesus told him, 'Go and do likewise.'"

—Luke 10:36-37

Last week we gained perspective on how much we have. This week, we will take that information and look at what the scriptures say about people who have what we have. Wealth is not sinful but it can lead to many sins. This week we will learn about how to turn our wealth into a blessing instead of a curse. So, armed with budgets and fresh perspective, let's dive into the word of God!

When you hear the word "neighbor" what do you think? Jesus defines neighbor for us in the parable of the Good Samaritan. It has nothing to do with where they live or what they have in common with us. In fact, it's not about them at all. It's about us. The neighbor is the one who helped the one that was hurting. Thus, the question is not "Who is my neighbor?" Instead we should ask, "Am I a neighbor?"

First, we must realize that "out of sight, out of mind" will not be an acceptable excuse. The decisions that we make with our wealth have eternal consequences for us and our neighbors no matter how far away they live.

Take a moment to read and reflect on Matthew 25:31-46. This week's goal is heart change that leads to life change. If we can change our minds and think about money, possessions and time as God does, then we can start to live like sheep instead of stubborn goats. We can start to impact the world for God in ways that we never could have imagined.

Our brothers and sisters in the third world live amazingly sacrificial lives. We'll travel to Africa and see how "rich" Christians live when surrounded by poverty. We'll have to confront this very difficult question: Is God's standard for them any different than his standard for us?

IF YOU LIVED IN AFRICA...

This week we will visit a few of our sister churches in Africa to see what life as a disciple would be like there. Can you imagine how different your life would be if you were born on the planet's second largest continent? Civil war, infectious disease, kidnapping, corruption and poverty cast a shadow on daily life for many Africans. Our brothers and sisters in Christ have a great task before them to evangelize their villages, towns and nations. They are a true light in a dark place. Yet, they are not immune to the hardships that come with living in Africa.

As a professor, Moise Konate is one of the more wealthy disciples in the church in Abidjan, Ivory Coast. Even with a high-profile job, he has to work at multiple colleges and endure difficult commutes to earn the $2,000 per month he needs to support his wife and four daughters. If you were to visit his apartment you would meet more than just his family. They are always housing and feeding disciples in need so there are often 10 people staying in their 3-bedroom flat. After the civil war that erupted in his country a few years ago his home served as a makeshift refugee camp for displaced Christians and their families. With all of these serious responsibilities Moise keeps his joy by playing guitar in the church band. His wife Marthe and his oldest daughter sing in the choir. He spends the little free time he has helping those who are struggling financially or spiritually.

Being wealthy or middle class in Africa is very different than the first world. Because poverty is within arm's reach instead of an ocean away, the relatively wealthy disciples like Moise embrace their role as Christians who have more than the people around them. Christ's commands are clear. Moise gives to all who have need. If you lived in Africa, even if you were just as wealthy as you are now, how different would your life be? The conviction from the Scriptures that you will gain this week will bring you closer to having first world wealth with a third world heart. Christ can connect us across oceans and cultures by the power of his word!

MISSION CHALLENGES

This week's mission challenges are all about adding conviction to last week's perspective. How third world can you be? Look over this list and decide which challenges you and your family may want to take on this week. Don't worry about doing the challenges on different days. Try to do as many as you can to the best of your ability.

Day 7
One plate, one cup, one set of silverware for one week. See how much simpler your life becomes when you use less stuff. Have everyone in your family pick their favorites.

Day 8
Make a giveaway bag for a beggar. In a reusable shopping bag include snack bars, Gatorade, socks and other supplies. Keep it in your car so you'll be at the ready. Don't forget a church invitation card!

Day 9
Perform a random act of selflessness. Some ideas: Pay for the person in line behind you. Give someone a card at church. Or offer to babysit for free.

Day 10
Have a garage sale that simplifies your life and earns money for special missions or a charity. You'll save, serve and simplify at the same time.

Day 11
Fast from social networks and pray for social justice. Take a day off from Facebook and Twitter. Pray every time you get the urge to check your feed.

Day 12
Tell a family member or friend what you've been learning from this passport and use the conversation as a springboard to share with them about Jesus and your church.

FAMILY NIGHT DEVOTIONAL

Sing

Scripture Deuteronomy 6:1-19

Discuss Read through the passage and discuss. Talk to your children about how you make your money and what you spend your money on (fun!). Show them what a budget is. Obviously this discussion needs to be tailored for their ages. Is there any possession that you take for granted?

Activity Have each family member choose their favorite plate, bowl, cup and utensils. This will be the only dishes used by the family for the week.

Game What's missing? Take turns having each family member go into a room and take an item away. Let the rest of the family go in and try to figure out what's missing. Do we have so much stuff that we don't even recognize when things are missing?

Pray Pray a prayer of gratitude for all that God has blessed your family with.

RECIPE OF THE WEEK

This week's recipe comes from Moise himself, who admits he is not a great cook. Luckily the link takes you to a 5-star version of this delicious and cost-effective comfort food: **Peanut Butter Stew**. Feel free to substitute or eliminate ingredients to make the recipe easier.

Ingredients
Peanut oil or vegetable oil
1 red onion, chopped
2 cloves garlic
2 Tbsps ginger
1 pound chicken (optional)
1 Tbsp crushed red pepper
Salt and ground black pepper
5 cups chicken stock
3 small sweet potatoes
1 16 oz. can chopped tomatoes
¼ pound collard greens
1 cup chunky peanut butter

landofenough.com/recipes

DAY 7:
GOD'S

What if I truly understood that all of my possessions are God's?

SCRIPTURE

Deuteronomy 6:1-19

"When you eat and are satisfied, be careful."

MISSION CHALLENGE

One plate, one cup, one set of silverware for one week. See how much simpler your life becomes when you use less stuff. Have everyone in your family pick their favorites.

IT'S ALL GOD'S...SERIOUSLY

We have to be honest. If we are in the wealthy half it is because God has placed us there. Just as those below the poverty line have been placed there by God. We'll get into why God does this later this week, but for now just let that idea really sink in. Your wealth and status have little to do with how awesome you are. God has put you where you are and given you what you have.

As we read through the text of Deuteronomy, we learn a great deal about the heart of God. He wants us to live long, prosper and multiply. He wants his people to be in a good land. This necessitates that there are lands that are not so good.

He gives the Israelites simple commands that will help them prosper, and they have nothing to do with money or things. They are to love God and teach their children to do the same. We can't control what kind of family we were born into but we can control the kind of family our children are born into and brought up in. By obeying this we can have a multi-generational impact for God!

God goes on to remind the Israelites that the land they are entering is set up for them by him. He expresses the same concern as Agur. If they lose sight of where their good things came from they might forget God. God then reveals a piece of his character: He is a jealous God. Loving the stuff he gave you more than him is a recipe for disaster. We cling to the Bible's promises but there are also some that we should avoid at all costs. God promises here that if we forget him because of our wealth, he will wipe us off the face of the earth. How's that for a promise!

REFLECT AND WRITE

Okay, so it is God's house that he's letting you use. What would he want you to do with it? Can you think of any scriptures that tell you what God would want or give examples of Christians using their homes for God?

It's God's car. (You worked really hard to buy it but it's still because of him.) What does God want you to do with his car?

It's God's time. How does God want you to spend his time?

It's God's money. What would God have you do with his money? Think about all that God has given you. Are you managing it like he would? Or are you using it primarily for yourself and your family?

ACT

If you were to rent a car or an apartment, part of the lease agreement would be an "acceptable use policy" detailing what uses are okay. Choose a few of your most cherished possessions and write an acceptable use policy for them. What would God deem a righteous use of the things he has given you?

Web Link
Visit some of our African churches. Where would you sleep?

Snap the QR code with your smartphone or visit www.landofenough.com

Do you understand the Bible's perspective on wealth?

SCRIPTURE

Matthew 19:16-30
1 Timothy 6:6-19
James 5:1-6

MISSION CHALLENGE

Make a giveaway bag for a beggar. In a reusable shopping bag include snack bars, Gatorade, socks and other supplies. Keep it in your car so you'll be at the ready. Don't forget to give a church invitation card.

WEALTH IS A ~~BLESSING~~ TRAP

Our society views wealth as blessing. To put it in caveman speak: rich good, poor bad. But what does God's word tell us to think about wealth? Money itself is neutral, neither good nor bad. It's the way we use money and our hearts toward it that count in God's eyes. The Bible has clear conviction for those who have a lot of money. Instead of wealth being a blessing, the Bible gives us a warning. Instead of encouraging us to aspire to great wealth, the Bible warns us of a trap.

These scriptures are just a sampling of the Bible's consistent warnings about the dangers of wealth. When we plan our futures we have to decide if we want to play with fire. Society propels us up the corporate ladder. We get news of raises and greater benefits and rejoice. But are these "blessings" really just the thorns of life tightening their stranglehold?

If we could take a wide-angle view of all of the opportunities, raises and bonuses we receive over the course of our lives, how much would our perspective change?

In a society as wealthy as ours, this is one of the most difficult concepts in the Bible for us to accept. How could our great wealth be a bad thing? We can be quick to warp or dismiss the Bible's clear teaching. Indeed, entire churches have been trapped by the false, "prosperity gospel."

Our third world brothers and sisters like Moise and Marthe avoid the trap of wealth by being wealthy toward the poor all around them.

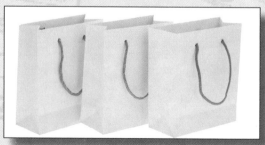

REFLECT AND WRITE

If you agree with God's warnings about wealth, then how much danger are you in? If you really took to heart the scriptures on wealth, what attitudes would you change to protect your heart and soul? What does your example teach your children about wealth? Is your example consistent with the Bible's teaching?

Why has God given you the wealth you have if it is so dangerous?

ACT

Corporations have entire departments devoted to risk management. They are responsible for making sure the company doesn't do anything foolish that puts it in danger of financial ruin. Assess your risk. How much danger are you in because of your wealth? Write down something you could do to manage your risk. Do you really need everything you have? Would you be comfortable with a downgraded lifestyle? Or, can you handle Jesus' challenge to the rich about how hard it is for them to enter the kingdom of God? Decide today if you can walk the line or if it would be better to start a retreat from wealth. Next week we'll talk about how to manage the risk of wealth effectively.

> **Web Link**
> *You'll be surprised to learn that this famous family gave away everything.*
>
> *Snap the QR code with your smartphone or visit www.landofenough.com*

DAY 9:
DARK SIDE

Have you been taken in by the dark side of wealth?

SCRIPTURE

Ephesians 5:1-7
Philippians 2:1-5
2 Timothy 3:1-5

MISSION CHALLENGE

Perform a random act of selflessness. Some ideas: Pay for the person in line behind you. Give someone a card at church. Or offer to babysit for free. Visit someone in the church who is struggling with health problems.

GREED, SELFISHNESS AND THE LOVE OF PLEASURE

The epic movies that we love share a similar plot point. In *Star Wars* and *The Lord of the Rings* we see good people with a lot of potential locked in a battle between dark and light. Darth Vader and Gollum stand out as losers in the battle of good and evil. In both cases, something morally neutral but powerful (the force, the ring of power) ends up ruling and ruining their lives. Likewise, wealth is morally neutral but extremely powerful.

It's in our nature to judge some sins as more serious than others. What would your hierarchy look like? If it reflects our society, then sins like greed, selfishness and the love of pleasure land near the bottom if they even make the list at all.

Today's passages look at why wealth can be so dangerous. The bottom line is this: wealth is dangerous because it is attached to a deadly host of sins that threaten our souls.

In contrast, Christianity is founded on self-sacrifice. As we read in Ephesians, Jesus "gave himself up for us as a fragrant offering and sacrifice to God." Our society is largely founded upon individualism and self-centeredness. When Paul warns Timothy of the sins of the last days, his 2000-year-old warning sounds eerily like our world today. People are lovers of themselves, lovers of pleasure, lovers of money and ungrateful. Selfishness and greed have become accepted and expected sins. Greed is simply shrewd resourcefulness. Selfishness is the way to financial independence. Pleasure at all costs becomes the goal of our lives while we miss out on true joy.

As disciples of Jesus, we need look no further than the cross to see that selfishness has NO place in Christianity.

REFLECT AND WRITE

Have these sins become more acceptable or less alarming than God's word tells us they should be? Can you think of a way that you have been greedy in the past? Have you been disguising selfishness with more friendly descriptions like "me time"? Looking back at week one, does your spending on luxuries point to a love of pleasure?

In your thinking, go one step further. God does expect us to work and have income. We do need time away and time with God that isn't selfish. We are supposed to enjoy our lives. How can we know if these parts of life are becoming sinful? Should we just give up trying? Should we sell everything and have nothing? There is a great temptation to be fatalistic. But, there is a better way to avoid these sins that are associated with wealth. We will talk about it in depth next week. But until then, what do you think is the right response to a lesson like this?

ACT

You've made a budget and a schedule. Now it's time to search the budget for hints of greed, selfishness and the love of pleasure. Look at what your schedule says about your heart. Your budget and schedule should reflect a purposeful outflow of everything that God puts into you. They should show tangible ways that you invite God to work in your life.

Web Link
Are you working too much?

Snap the QR code with your smartphone or visit www.landofenough.com

41

DAY 10:
WORLDLINESS

In what ways has worldliness crept into your heart?

SCRIPTURE

1 John 2:15-17
Galatians 6:14
Luke 9:25

MISSION CHALLENGE

Have a garage sale that simplifies your life and earns money for special missions or a charity. You'll save, serve and simplify at the same time. You will also free up space to actually park your car in the garage.

DO NOT LOVE THE WORLD

In the Bible, we often read about the line God has drawn between *sarx* and *pneuma* or flesh and spirit. As society evolves, the line seems more unclear. However, the danger of worldliness and the blessing of spirituality remain unchanged.

The Bible's stance on worldliness is clear: "Do not love the world." In the HCSB we are warned in this same passage against taking "pride in one's lifestyle." Worldliness and wealth are inextricably linked. C.J. Mahaney defines worldliness as "love for this fallen world," saying, "It's loving the values and pursuits of the world that stand opposed to God. It rejects God's rule and replaces it with our own. It elevates our sinful desires for the things of this fallen world above God's commands and promises."

Worldliness is seductive and cunning as it works on our hearts. It tempts us to blur lines and sear our consciences. Satan, called "the ruler of the kingdom of the air," wants us to worship the things of this world. This was one of his tactics with Jesus as he tempted him in the desert.

Worldliness takes many forms, making it hard to detect and keep a handle on. Like a weed that you pull in one place only to discover in another, worldliness can pop up in many places in our lives. So we must be vigilant and look in all the nooks and crannies of our hearts. Unfortunately, living in a wealthy society increases the temptation for worldliness in many ways.

When we look to the African disciples we see a great example. Instead of being overcome by the world, they are changing the world by being selfless even as they have great need. They live kingdom-focused lives.

REFLECT AND WRITE

Are there areas of your life that are worldly instead of spiritual? Think about the shows you watch on television. What are you doing when you are online? Looking at things you could buy? What kind of music do you listen to? Are you focused on the newest and best products or technologies? Why do you use social networking sites? What do your statuses and comments reflect about God? Do you dress with modesty? These are just a few areas where worldliness can creep into our lives.

ACT

Pray and think about any other ways that worldliness may have crept into your life.

Battle back from the brink by taking a serious stand against worldliness. Cut out activities and habits that look more like the world than the spirit. Clean out your music. Stop rationalizing the shows you watch. Pray to be content with what you have. You'll immediately have more time for the things of God. You can't become a spiritual person with one foot in the world.

Web Link
What would happen if you quit Face-book?

Snap the QR code with your smartphone or visit www.landofenough.com

DAY 11:
INJUSTICE

What is the solution to the injustice in our world?

SCRIPTURE

Leviticus 19:15
Psalm 140:12
Proverbs 29:7
Matthew 23:23

MISSION CHALLENGE

Fast from social networks and pray for social justice. Take a day off from Facebook and Twitter. Pray every time you get the urge to check your feed.

THE DEFENDER OF THE HELPLESS

Many Christians today have a growing passion for justice and fairness. Fairness is something that we demand in our own lives. Few things will discourage us more than a sense of unfair treatment. Followers of Christ are challenged to take that indignation and apply it to others. Do you only apply the scriptures about justice and fairness to yourself?

We have to face the fact that we live in an unfair world. The deck is stacked against billions of people from their first breath to their last. Sometimes it seems like we are afraid to ask God hard questions out of fear. But God can handle tough questions. And this is one that our study necessitates: God, why is the world so unjust?

Moise wrestled with this question as his country spiralled into a revolution that he had no control of. One day there was order, the next day there was chaos.

We see in these scriptures and many more (do a concordance search for "justice") that God is just. God is fair. He hates injustice. He cares about and looks after the poor, orphans and widows. The people we often pity actually hold a special place in the heart of God. Maybe they should pity us.

It's one thing for God to be just, but what of his followers? Do we love justice? Do we desire a world where everyone gets a fair shake? Right now in our world there are discrimination, human trafficking, physical abuse, abandonment and other forms of injustice that break God's heart minute by minute.

We are God's plan to end injustice. But nothing will change if our hearts aren't soft and moved to action.

44

REFLECT AND WRITE

Imagine a world where everyone got a fair start. What would be different? Would life be easier or more difficult for you? Is there any injustice or unfairness in your life that you turn a blind eye to? What can we do when we see injustice?

We may be tempted to politicize this but we must avoid taking political positions in favor of taking a spiritual position. Politics and the heart of God rarely intersect on either side of the aisle. Do you share God's heart in this area?

ACT

Decide to be a fair person. Look for people who have less than you and treat them with respect. Look to donate money or time to an aid organization that promotes justice in the world. Many of them are not necessarily Christian because mainline Christianity tends to de-emphasize the Bible's teaching on injustice for the poor. Pray for justice and fairness in our world.

Web Link
How much do 85 people own?
Meet HOPE Worldwide.

Snap the QR code with your smartphone or visit
www.landofenough.com

DAY 12:
DO SOMETHING

What happens when we fail to act?

SCRIPTURE

James 4:13-17

Haggai 1:2-5

THE SIN OF OMISSION

Ready for some rocket science? Doing nothing will do nothing.

Doing something could change the world. Now that we've seen God's heart toward our wealth we have to make a decision. Will we do something or nothing? Maybe you've already thrown up your hands in frustration because the teaching seems so hard. Don't give up. You don't have to do everything, but you do have to do something.

The concept behind James 4:17 has been given a label by theologians. It is called the sin of omission. The idea is that you sin by not doing something, as opposed to the sins of commission that we commit with our actions. Murder and adultery are terrible sins of commission. Sins like laziness and apathy are just as hurtful to God and people and they occur when we fail to act. Now that we know where we stand and what God wants, we have to act. We have to do something.

The people in Haggai's day were charged with rebuilding God's temple. They stalled for various reasons as they built up their own homes and their own lives. They wondered why they weren't being blessed by God. They weren't doing what God put them on the planet to do. Next week we will look at the positive side of all of this. Loving money is bad. We have a lot of money. So what are we supposed to do? There's no one-size-fits-all-answer to that question except this: do something!

It's amazing how hardship can cause us to act. The disciples in Acts spread the word around the globe because of persecution. Disciples in Africa use every hardship as an opportunity to share the goodness of God.

REFLECT AND WRITE

What have you been doing to serve the poor and needy and impact our world? Can you think of some ways that you may have neglected the poor by doing nothing? What if everyone in the rich half of the world just did something to help the poor half?

Maybe you are not in frequent contact with the economically needy. All of us face spiritually needy people all of the time. Are you quick to act on the spiritual needs that you see? As a disciple of Jesus you are uniquely qualified to change a person's eternal destiny.

ACT

Sometimes we fail to act because we don't see the needs around us. Hopefully this passport is highlighting the great needs of the churches we support around the world. We also have to open our eyes to the people all around us in our churches, workplaces, schools and homes.

Resolve to be the kind of disciple that always does something whenever you see someone who needs the love of Christ.

Web Link
Start doing something in your area right now.

Snap the QR code with your smartphone or visit www.landofenough.com

REST AND REFLECT

USE THIS SPACE TO REVIEW
THIS WEEK'S LESSONS AND
TAKE NOTES ON SUNDAY'S
SERMON.

WEEK THREE

BOUNDARIES

BOUNDARIES

"There are those who move boundary stones; they pasture flocks they have stolen. They drive away the orphan's donkey and take the widow's ox in pledge. They thrust the needy from the path and force all the poor of the land into hiding." —Job 24:2-4

In chapter 24, Job offers a heartbreaking lament to his friends. He describes the plight of the poor and the wickedness of sin. In the end, the mighty are brought low by God and justice is meted out. In verse 2, Job offers an insightful perspective on why there is such disparity. He says that we move boundary stones to get what we want from those who have less. In biblical times, property and possessions were literally marked by stones as the boundaries. A wicked person could easily go out to the edge of his field and gain more land from his neighbor by simply kicking the stone. With a little effort we can see how perfectly this concept applies to the rich and poor of our day.

We may not have literal boundary stones but we have other kinds of boundaries or markers for our wealth. We have income, credit, property, possessions and time, as we've seen. All of these are boundaries that we can set limits on. Our society scoffs at boundaries with such things. Why would we want to limit our wealth? Shouldn't we just keep kicking the stone until we have as much as possible? Such an attitude runs afoul of the convictions we gained last week and provides no solution for the disparity we saw in week one.

If we are willing to cap our wealth and lifestyle by setting boundaries, we start to fall in line with some of the biblical principles we learned last week. God's standard for wealth no longer becomes an impossibility. We actually see it as his money, time or possession so we ask him how much we should keep. Then we set a boundary on the rest. We will probably (even hopefully) make more than our boundary. Great! That extra is the amount that God has entrusted us to distribute! What an amazing responsibility and opportunity God has placed in the hands of wealthy people like us.

So this week you get to decide where you will set your wealth boundary. Will you keep moving the stone to the detriment of the fatherless, the widows and the poor or will your boundary result in great impact for those in need? As they say, with rolling stones you can't get no satisfaction!

IF YOU LIVED IN CYPRUS...

Dylan and Ann Mathias lead our sister church in Limassol, Cyprus. Cyprus is a small island nation in the Mediterranean Sea on the border of Europe and the Middle East. As Dylan will tell you, it is the site of the first-ever church planting in history (See Acts 13:1-4). Currently we have 13 brothers and sisters in Cyprus. Dylan and Ann, like many of our small church leaders around the world, work full-time secular jobs and lead the church. Because of the kingdom focus and generosity of the Mathiases and the other church members, they are able to rent a building in the center of the city to hold their services and meetings. Dylan is actually a British citizen and doesn't know how long he'll be in Cyprus for his job but as long as he is there, he wants to have a great impact and lead God's people.

None of this would be possible if they were using their wealth, career, status and time for themselves. If Dylan was focused on his advancement and his family he would use his time and money very differently. But he is focused on the kingdom's advancement and God's family. He uses his vacation time to go to retreats and get training. Last fall he brought his entire family to the U.S. for three weeks to learn how to be a more effective small church leader (and someday a large church leader!). All of this was with his own money and initiative.

Even though the church is quite small, they have big dreams for God and the island of Cyprus. Their dream is to have 5 churches on the island by 2020. And with the sacrificial example of Dylan and Ann, the disciples are motivated to see their dream for God's kingdom come true.

When we decide to limit ourselves so that God can have more of our time and resources, God's kingdom can grow just like Jesus said it would: from the smallest of seeds, to a tree that even the birds can make homes in.

MISSION CHALLENGES

Our mission challenges for week three allow us to experience life with boundaries. Instead of just going with the flow, these challenges allow you to experience life lived on purpose. Read through the list below so you can make plans to do as many challenges as possible. Have fun and get the whole family involved whenever possible!

Day 13
Fill up a giveaway box. Put seldom-used clothing, appliances and technology in a box that you can donate to a non-profit or give away to people you know. Can you fill it each month?

Day 14
Go dark to bring more light into your life. Go off grid and use no power in your house for a full day. No lights, no AC, but a lot of quality time with God and family.

Day 15
Pray three times a day. In the Bible, Jews prayed at 9 a.m., noon and 3 p.m. Set your phone alarm to remind you to stop and pray for world missions or your charity three times a day.

Day 16
Have a "no spend" day. Pick a day and resolve to spend $0. No money comes out of your account, no cash and no credit. It's harder than you think.

Day 17
Have a change week. Keep a tally of all of the change you get from your purchases (cash or credit). Add the total to your special missions contribution or charity.

Day 18
Have a mountaintop prayer. Go to a high place like a hill or a parking garage and pray about sacrificing now but experiencing heaven someday.

FAMILY NIGHT DEVOTIONAL

Sing

Scripture Joshua 1:7

Discuss What does it mean to be careful to obey God? What would turning to the right or to the left look like? Is there any practice that your family has that is not on track with God? Humbly ask your children what they think. Talk about important boundaries you have set for your family.

Activity Have everyone draw a picture of a straight path. On each side of the path write or draw things that can derail us.

Game Take turns trying to find each other with blindfolds on. Put obstacles in the way and have the family yell "right" and "left" to keep people from hitting the obstacles. Have some people being a good voice and others give false information.

Pray!

RECIPE OF THE WEEK

Fasolia is a versatile dish centered around inexpensive white beans. You can buy cheaper dry white beans and soak overnight or quicker canned white beans. This recipe makes a great side or main dish. If you like spice you can add your favorite hot sauce.

Ingredients
2 cups white beans
2 carrots, peeled and sliced
1 potato, cut into chunks
Salt and pepper to taste
5 Tbsps olive oil
1-2 lemons (juice)
1/2 a cup chopped parsley
1 medium onion, quartered

landofenough.com/recipes

DAY 13:
FREEDOM

Are you living within the boundaries God has set?

SCRIPTURE

Job 38:1-11

Joshua 1:7

Acts 17:26

Galatians 5:1,16

MISSION CHALLENGE

Fill up a giveaway box. Put seldom-used clothing, appliances and technology in a box that you can donate to a nonprofit or give away to people you know. Can you fill it four times a year and give it away?

BOUNDARIES BRING FREEDOM

When we hear about boundaries our independent spirits can easily become riled. We want freedom to do what we want, when we want, with what we have! But let's be honest about where that really gets us. There is even a credit card out there called the "freedom" card. I wonder how many people using the freedom card feel free. How many have used their freedom to wrack up a great deal of crippling debt? How many wish they could make an impact with their money but are only able to make a minimum payment?

Our possessions provide similar shackles. We think that if we had this or that we would be happy. We buy the boat or the house with the bigger yard and we end up having to clean and prep the boat. We spend more time on the lawn mower. We become slaves to the things that we own. We have to maintain our possessions. Thus, more possessions often equals less time. That doesn't sound like freedom.

Here's the reality: Regardless of our desire for freedom, God is a God of boundaries. Within those boundaries we find true freedom.

In these passages, we see that God has set boundaries from the very beginning. When natural boundaries are violated bad things happen like floods and wildfires. When spiritual boundaries are violated the results are similarly disastrous. God has set boundaries for where we live. So if you live in the wealthy half, that's his plan for you. But he hasn't put us here, in the land of the free, to be wanton and fleshly. True freedom comes when we do not turn to the right or the left from the spiritual boundaries God has put in place.

REFLECT AND WRITE

How much do you really need? Imagine if you had 20% less income, time and possessions. How would that change your focus and priorities? What would get cut out?

If you purposely limited yourself by 20% so you could give the extra away would you really miss it? How would your life be enriched by such a boundary? How would others benefit?

ACT

Take a look at your budget from week one. If you still haven't made a budget stop everything you are doing and do it now! Remember, not being responsible with our money and time is a sin against God.

Once you have created your budget, move your wealth boundary stone by experimenting with different incomes. (This is easier if you made your budget on a computer spreadsheet.) If you made $500 less per month what would you cut out? What about $1000 less? Are the things you would cut out essential? Could you make it with less income?

Web Link
See what's happening in Cyprus.
Get on a budget!

Snap the QR code with your smartphone or visit
www.landofenough.com

DAY 14:
WEALTH CAP

How much of my wealth do I really need to keep for myself?

SCRIPTURE

Acts 2:42-47

Acts 4:32-37

Acts 5:1-11

2 Corinthians 8:1-5

MISSION CHALLENGE

Go dark to bring more light into your life. Go off grid and use no power in your house for a full day (except for the refrigerator). No lights, no air condition, but a lot of quality time with God and family.

SETTING UP A WEALTH BOUNDARY

In this passport we have looked at wealth, poverty, injustice, greed, simplicity, budgeting, scheduling and many other things. We can boil all of those subjects down into **one easy-to-grasp decision**. One choice can go a long way toward guarding your heart from the trap of wealth. One conviction can actually make an impact on the world's poorest. One firm decision can change your whole outlook on wealth. That one choice is a wealth boundary.

It isn't an easy choice, just a simple one. A wealth boundary, or **a cap on how much of your income you will spend on yourself and your family**, answers almost every hard question we've asked so far in this series. A wealth boundary cries out, "enough is enough"! It agrees with God that everything you have is his. It serves as a warning against the deceitful trap of wealth. It tamps our tendencies toward greed, selfishness and love of pleasure by setting limits where society has none. It gives us less opportunity to become worldly; indeed, a wealth boundary is quite otherworldly. It is a thoughtful response to the question we like to avoid about why we have so much while others suffer unjustly with so little. It also keeps us from the sin of doing nothing as we give away our more than enough with great joy and peace. Oh, and as today's passages show, it looks a lot like how our first-century family helped each other and spread the gospel all over the world in one generation.

This same spirit of discipline and sacrifice is alive and well in our small, self-supporting churches. It's up to us to follow their example and see how God uses our self-imposed limits to cause his word to spread without limit as we cheerfully give!

REFLECT AND WRITE

How would a wealth boundary change your life? What effect would it have on your family? Be sure to list any negatives and positives that you see. How would you use your extra money to impact the world? If you made more money but kept the same wealth boundary imagine how much more you could do and how much trouble you could avoid. What will your friends and family think of your lifestyle and refusal to keep up with the Joneses?

Imagine if your entire church decided to set wealth boundaries. How many resources would be freed up to grow God's kingdom and impact the world? How much closer would the members become?

ACT

All right, this is it. Talk with your spouse if you are married. Pray. **Set your wealth boundary.** This won't be perfect right off the bat. You may need to adjust as you continue to follow your budget in the coming weeks and months. Having a plan is a great first step. Pray for perseverance and great impact.

Web Link
Are you dying of "stuffocation"?

Snap the QR code with your smartphone or visit www.landofenough.com

DAY 15:
TIME BOUNDARY

What are you
doing here?

SCRIPTURE

Ecclesiastes 12:1-8
Psalm 103:13-16
Isaiah 40:6-8
Luke 12:20

MISSION CHALLENGE

Pray three times a day. In the Bible, Jews prayed at 9 a.m., noon and 3 p.m. Set your phone alarm to remind you to stop and pray for world missions three times a day.

TIME IS OF THE ESSENCE

When we talk about boundaries, we must first recognize the boundaries that God has built into his creation. We live in a world in which time is always moving forward. That time is limited. There is a boundary set by God determining how long we will live. Only he knows when our time will be up. Life is short. The Scriptures talk frequently of the boundary of time.

We don't like to think about the boundary of death and we certainly shouldn't dwell on it but it can do a lot of good to think about the brevity of our time here every so often. We are limited by time every day. Every time we meet up with people we are limited. We even refer to it as "spending" time because we can't have it back. We are limited in time with our spouses and our children. We are often left with little time to spend doing what we really want to do for God, our families and ourselves.

With a wealth boundary we can be sure that we will not waste our wealth. In the same way, goals and dreams for the future can guard against wasting the precious time we have been given by God. In 1 Corinthians 9, Paul tells the Corinthians that he does not run aimlessly. Our futures are ultimately determined by God but that doesn't mean we shouldn't plan and dream as we seek his will. When Elijah falls into depression in 1 Kings 19, God asks him twice, "What are you doing here?" I think God may be asking many of us the same question. Do you know the answer?

In Cyprus, free time is spent building family as a church. Most of the members are from different countries so extra effort is needed to form bonds. Picnics and retreats fill their schedules with joy.

60

REFLECT AND WRITE

What do you think God wants you to do with your life? Is there a big dream that he has put on your heart? What goals do you need to make to see that dream realized? Have you talked to trusted disciples about your dreams? Great dreams don't have to be elaborate. Do you dream of having a Christian marriage, raising your children to be disciples or becoming a minister or elder, whether paid or not? Your dream may not be to serve in the ministry but rather to fund missionaries as you serve your home church. What does God want you to do in the limited time you've got?

ACT

Look back at the schedule you made in week one or a recent calendar. What does the way you spend your time say about your priorities? If someone else looked at your schedule, what would they say your dreams and goals might be? Now, take the goals and dreams you imagined and be the boss of your time. How much time should you spend with God, family and whatever else is necessary to see your goals accomplished and your dreams come true? Remember to stay flexible to God's will. Keeping your goals in mind will radically change the way you spend your limited time!

Web Link
Here's how you really spend your time.

Snap the QR code with your smartphone or visit www.landofenough.com

DAY 16:
STUFF LIMIT

How much stress are my possessions bringing into my life?

SCRIPTURE

Ecclesiastes 2:4-11

Daniel 4:28-37

GETTING THINGS UNDER CONTROL

It might take a while to feel the effects, but setting wealth and time boundaries is going to give you so much freedom. There is one more boundary that the wealthy of our day must set in order to leave anxiety, pressure and guilt behind. We have to limit our stuff. The self-storage business in the United States made $22 billion dollars last year alone. There are even TV shows devoted to how much extra we have. While they may be entertaining, they don't cast a positive light on our excessiveness.

Many of us have a basement or a garage or an attic (or all three) full of things that we rarely use. There is no way to measure the low-level stress that stuff and clutter cause. Being free of excess brings freedom and joy. As an example, think about how stressful it is to search and search for something you can't locate. Many times, we can't find things because we have so many other things. Also, when we sell or give away our extra things we can benefit many people as we free up our lives.

In these passages, we see that great wealth, fame and possessions get us nowhere. Yet our society is bent on more, more, more. The experience of Nebuchadnezzar is intriguing. At the height of his power he is sent to the countryside with nothing. His fame, pride and wealth kept him from realizing the one thing he really needed. After seven years he prayed to God and was restored to power. God was all he really needed.

When we don't stay on top of what we buy and what we keep we can really lose track of God.

REFLECT AND WRITE

Take a walk through your cluttered areas. What haven't you used in the last year? Think about the gadgets and tech stuff you have. Do you really need those things? Do they actually make your life better? How would things be better if you simplified? Could anyone else benefit more from the things you have? What process do you go through before buying something? Do you get advice, pray and truly consider if it is a need?

ACT

Find a bin or make a pile to start putting your excess stuff in. Decide if you want to donate it or have a garage sale. Contact anyone who might be in need. Decide that you will not have cluttered areas in your house/life. Don't forget to look through your clothes, kid's toys and kitchenware. Set an alarm in your digital calendar that reminds you to declutter every six months or so.

Web Link
Pro tips for dejunking your life.

Snap the QR code with your smartphone or visit www.landofenough.com

63

DAY 17:
TRUE RICHES

By what standard do I measure the richness of my life?

SCRIPTURE
Mark 10:17-31

MISSION CHALLENGE

Have a change week. Keep a tally of all of the change you get from your purchases (cash or credit). Add the total to your special missions contribution or charity.

THE RICHEST PEOPLE IN THE WORLD

So far this week we've focused on how to set boundaries for our wealth. Today we will begin to look at why. The whole idea of setting boundaries is uncomfortable and foreign to our society. Yet the benefits are incredible in this life (as we will see today) and the next (as we will see tomorrow).

After the rich young ruler goes away sad, Peter and the disciples feel quite hopeless. If such a righteous and zealous man could be disqualified for lacking one thing, how could they be sure of their standing with God? Jesus' words reassure them even as they might unsettle us. For how many of us, during the course of this study, would have to admit that we are much more like the rich man than the disciples who left everything?

The promise for those who give is that they will get. And they will get 100 times more. Jesus isn't just telling them to hold on for heaven. The promise is for this life. That is an awesome promise even in spite of the persecution added in. Now, this doesn't mean we'll be rich and win the lottery or any of that prosperity gospel stuff.

The scriptures that we saw in Acts earlier this week show us clearly how God answered this promise. The early disciples gave away their extra so no one had unmet needs. Their wealth boundaries helped this blessing to be met. When God's church takes Jesus' teaching on wealth seriously this promise comes true. Only in the church of Christ can we have 100 mothers and fathers and homes as the church shares loving friendships and property and wealth. In this way the rich and poor alike are blessed by the same promise.

The members of the church in Cyprus pool together their money to lease a church building.

REFLECT AND WRITE

What have you given up for God's kingdom? In what ways has the kingdom provided many times more of whatever you gave up? Who are your brothers, sisters, mothers, fathers, children and fields?

Is there anything that you are afraid to give up? Trust in Jesus' promise so you can receive the blessings that come with cheerful and sacrificial giving.

Added onto the promises is the terrible promise of persecution. We should expect persecution and embrace it (although not seek it out). Are you afraid to give because you are afraid of persecution? Will friends and family start to question you if you sacrifice?

ACT

Make a list of your true riches. Write down the names of your fathers and mothers and possessions in God's kingdom. Praise God for each of the blessings that undoubtedly add up to make you the richest person in the world.

Web Link
What would change if you didn't have the Internet at home?

Snap the QR code with your smartphone or visit www.landofenough.com

DAY 18:
ETERNITY

Do I allow the dream of eternity with God to inspire my life on earth?

SCRIPTURE

Hebrews 11:8-19

WEALTH THAT HAS NO BOUNDARY

In yesterday's reading we focused on the blessings that we get in this life when we give up our wealth in its various forms. After Jesus promises one hundredfold blessings in this life he adds an amazing promise, "...in the age to come eternal life." Today we will focus on that part of the promise.

Our passage gives us insight into the faithfully sacrificial life of Abraham. First, he must leave all the comfort and security of his homeland and his people. We are told that he was able to do this because he was looking forward to a heavenly city. He believed in the promise of God that his descendants would be as numerous as the stars. This wasn't a promise he'd ever get to see. But he wasn't focused on just his lifespan. He wanted to have lasting impact. The writer tells us that people like Abraham are strangers. They don't truly live in the here and now, in our time and place. They are focused on the place that God is preparing for them. This attitude allowed Abraham to be sacrificial to the utmost, as exemplified with Isaac on Mount Moriah. He was so focused on another world that he made up the idea of resurrection! He raised the knife and was blessed for his faith.

Unfortunately, many today see heaven as a false motive. They say they're not just doing this to get to heaven. To which we should yell, "Why not!" The next life is going to be amazing. It is a great motivator. It is a biblical promise so there's no false motive in it. On top of that there are many passages that encourage us to give now so we'll get in heaven. That's not works vs. faith, that's just what the Bible says! So let's close out this week by focusing on heaven.

REFLECT AND WRITE

What do you think heaven will be like? Close your eyes and imagine. Write down whatever words come to mind. Is there anything on this earth that you would trade for eternity with God? If you died right now are you confident that you are heaven bound? If not, talk to someone right away about getting right with God. Think about your faithfulness to God. Do you have enough faith to see yourself through to the end and never fall away from God? Never give up your life for anything that is not eternal.

ACT

Spend time praying to God about what he might be calling you to sacrifice. Is there something that may keep you from eternity with God? Is there something that may keep others from hearing the message of salvation? Ask God to put you on a path that leads heavenward with amazing impact all along the way.

REST AND REFLECT

USE THIS SPACE TO REVIEW
THIS WEEK'S LESSONS AND
TAKE NOTES ON SUNDAY'S
SERMON.

WEEK FOUR

MISSION

MISSION

"Those who had been scattered preached the word wherever they went." —Acts 8:4

We have this idea in our heads that being a missionary means going somewhere to spread the gospel. How easy it is to forget that we are all somewhere that needs the gospel. We send money and fund missionaries "over there" because we have resources that they do not have. But one thing that we do have in common with the places we support is lost people. Thus, our mission, their mission and the mission of Christ are the same. No matter where we are we "seek and...save the lost" (Luke 19:10).

This was the heart of the first Christians. No matter where they went or why they were there, they shared the gospel of Jesus. The result was that in one generation the entire world heard the gospel. Wherever there was a disciple there was a church. This same spirit has caused churches to be planted all over the world in our generation.

It may be jolting to jump from lessons on wealth boundaries to devotionals about evangelism, but the leap is essential. We can never become the kind of Christians or churches that send money overseas to missionaries but are not actually missionaries ourselves. Jesus called out such hypocrisy with unapologetic fervor, saying to the Pharisees, "You travel over land and sea to win a single convert, and when you have succeeded, you make them twice as much a son of hell as you are" (Matthew 23:15).

As we will see in this week's devotionals, our wealth and our lack of personal mission are more related than we might think. Comfort is a mission killer. The scattering that spread the seed of the gospel across the world in Acts 8 came because of persecution. The relative comfort of the early church was pulled out from under them. They proved to be true disciples by turning their hardship into an opportunity to share their faith.

Like them, are you committed to preaching the word wherever you go, even if the only places you go are a secular job, suburban home and exotic activities in your neighborhood? When it comes to mission, it's not a question of where you go but what you do right where you are.

IF YOU LIVED IN UKRAINE...

The Kiev Church Building On Fire

It's hard to avoid the news coming out of Ukraine these days but because of disciples on the mission not all of the news is bad.

The people of Ukraine have endured political unrest, revolution and an ongoing civil war. There is a cloud of uncertainty hanging over daily life. Our brothers and sisters have fought to be revolutionary Christians in the midst of the chaos by showing their fellow countrymen the love and peace of Jesus Christ. Instead of being defined by political parties or patriotism they have chosen to be defined by Christ and his mission. In the early days of the revolution one of our brothers was even killed in the chaos. That same week two people were baptized in Kiev.

Our brothers and sisters in Donetsk, nearest the fighting, had to temporarily evacuate their homes to avoid violence. They were welcomed into the homes of their church family and taken care of in Kiev. Like the early Christians who bore fruit wherever they went, the Christians in Ukraine have stayed focused on the mission despite great turmoil and suffering. In this way they have proven their devotion to Christ. If you woke up tomorrow to a new government, riots and civil unrest would your faith be rocked or would you be a rock because of your faith? Would you, like the Ukrainian disciples, use darkness as an opportunity to shine the bright light of Christ?

This week we'll go beyond giving to the mission and get back on the mission ourselves. Our Ukrainian brothers and sisters are a living example of mission-focused living. Let their testimony take away your excuses. Let their response to political revolution spark a spiritual revolution in your heart. The mission challenges this week are designed to stretch you and your family from your comfort zone to the place where God can use you for his mission, even if you never leave your area code.

MISSION CHALLENGES

These are truly mIssion challenges. Doing the mission is the best way to support the mission (and it's free!). Each challenge is associated with someone in the bible who got to experience God because a believer was willing to be bold. Who will get to experience God because of your boldness this week? Think about ways to get as many as possible involved in your evangelism.

Day 19
The Levi: Share your faith with someone who is at work like a cashier or a waitress. They're a captive audience! It will be good for your heart and theirs.

Day 20
The Apollos: Invite a friend or a couple over for dinner and tell them about your faith, your church and all that you've been learning this month.

Day 21
The Goliath: Share your faith with the most intimidating person you can think of. Pray for confidence and impact from your great big strong God.

Day 22
The Paul: Share your faith with someone by being interested in something they like. Maybe you already share a hobby or an activity with someone. Let them know about your love for Christ.

Day 23
The Barnabas: Take someone with you and share your faith. Pick a brother or sister or even one of your children to be your missionary partner.

Day 24
The Bartimaeus: Share your faith and more with someone who is in need. You could give food to a homeless person or help an elderly person with groceries. Be sure to also tell them about Jesus.

FAMILY NIGHT DEVOTIONAL

Sing

Scripture Jeremiah 20:9, Luke 19:1-10

Activity Buy some candy or something sweet. Start eating the candy right out of the bag without sharing any. Groan and say things like, "This is so good!"

Discuss While still chewing on the candy start to ask your family questions about how it makes them feel when you don't share. After a little while give them candy of their own and ask if it makes them happy. While they are enjoying their candy ask them if heaven is better than candy. Talk about how we must share our faith and the everlasting joy it brings to the Zaccheuses in our lives.

Craft Make invitations to church or an outreach event using paper, crayons and candy. Tape the candy to the invitation and write creative lines like "Come see how sweet God is." Make a list of friends to share your faith and your candy with.

Pray!

RECIPE OF THE WEEK

Holopchi (stuffed cabbage) is an inexpensive and hearty Ukrainian dish. To save time you can prepare the cabbage rolls in the morning and put them in a crock pot. You'll come home to a delicious smelling meal in the evening.

Ingredients
1 Tbsp butter
1 large onion, chopped
¾ pound ground pork
1/2 cup fresh bread crumbs
1 egg
2 teaspoons salt
1 teaspoon black pepper
1 head cabbage
2 cups chicken stock
1 Tbsp all-purpose flour
1 cup sour cream
1 Tbsp dill

landofenough.com/recipes

FRUIT

What does the fruit in my life say about the focus of my life?

SCRIPTURE

Matthew 7:15-23

John 15:1-8

2 Corinthians 13:5

MISSION CHALLENGE

The Levi: Share your faith with someone who is at work like a cashier or a waitress. They're a captive audience! It will be good for your heart and theirs.

BRANCHING OUT WITH THE GOSPEL

The concept that Jesus lays out in today's passages is easy to understand but hard to swallow. If you were walking in the woods and an oak tree tried to tell you that it was an apple tree the first thing you would do is freak out because you found a talking tree. The next thing you might do is examine the tree to see if its claim was true. If it is really an apple tree as it says, then where are the apples? Jesus says that we can judge ourselves in the exact same way. It doesn't matter how much we talk about Jesus. It's the fruit that counts. When you look at your life, are you producing Christian things? Are you bearing fruit for God?

There are many ways to bear fruit. Any time we make the world around us more Christlike we are bearing fruit for God. Perhaps the most significant way that we can bear fruit is by producing a whole other Christian who can then bear more fruit on their own.

Of course, this is not accomplished by our own effort alone. John's gospel says that when we remain in Jesus we will bear much fruit. It's promised. So what does it mean if we aren't bearing much fruit? Well, we have to judge a tree by its fruit and not by our feelings. If our tree bears no Christian fruit then can it be a Christian tree?

The church in Kiev was literally thrown into the fire. One of the halls where the church in Kiev met for services was burned down during a riot. Instead of being hindered by the burned-up chairs and Bibles, the church moved on with great faith, proving that they are rooted in Christ and not the comfort of their building.

REFLECT AND WRITE

Let's take the tree metaphor one step further. Christians are rooted in Christ and have a strong trunk that is not easily moved especially as we grow in Christ. Our branches are all of the places where we can reach out. What's on the end of your branches? Is there fruit being developed in the places where you could reach out or are your branches bare?

ACT

Write or draw a tree with a branch labeled for each of the places in your life that you regularly interact with lost people. (I.e.: work, neighborhood, kid's activities, hobbies and recreation.) At the end of each branch write down ways that God could work through you to bear fruit. Are there any people that may just be waiting for you to open your mouth and share the gospel? Pray through a plan to have a life that bears fruit on every level.

Web Link
Here's the latest news from the Kiev church.

Snap the QR code with your smartphone or visit www.landofenough.com

DAY 20:
FIRST LOVE

Are you
still in
the fight?

SCRIPTURE

Revelation 2:1-5
2 Samuel 1:27
Hebrews 3:14

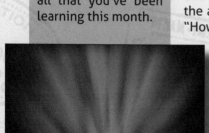

DO THE THINGS YOU DID AT FIRST

Of the seven churches in Revelation, we know the most about the church in Ephesus. Acts tells us that Paul started the church and stayed there for two years. There were great miracles and many conversions. There was even a public scroll burning by repentant sorcerers! One of the most touching moments in Acts is Paul's tear-filled farewell to the elders of Ephesus as he travels to Jerusalem. We also have the epistle to the Ephesians that ends with Paul including them among those who have an "undying love."

Revelation is written a few decades later and we get a very different picture of the church in Ephesus. Jesus praises them for persevering and remaining faithful but holds this against them: they have forsaken their first love. They have fallen far from their original zeal. He counsels them to repent and do the things they did at first.

As we grow older in Christ, it seems like the great commission of Jesus Christ is the easiest conviction to neglect. Like the Ephesians in Revelation we have persevered and endured but have we also stopped doing the things we did at first? Has the great commission become an inconvenient option in your life?

David's lament upon hearing the news of Saul and Jonathan's death sounds strikingly similar to the accusation of Jesus in Revelation 2:5. He says, "How the mighty have fallen! The weapons of war have perished!" (2 Samuel 1:27). Is Christ lamenting you or your church in the same way? Is Christ wondering when you will take up the sword of his word and fight for his kingdom again? "We have come to share in Christ, if indeed we hold our original conviction firmly to the very end."

REFLECT AND WRITE

Think about when you first became a Christian. What was it like?

Can you think of good things that you used to do but you are no longer doing? (I.e.: daily devotionals, Bible studies with friends, evangelism, serving, etc...)

A lot of times our lives change so quickly that our convictions can't catch up. With every transition (like going from single to married or from college to a full-time job) we have to rework our lives so that we can still do the things we did at first even if we do them in a different way. Just because we aren't on a college campus doesn't mean we shouldn't share our faith; we might just have to do it differently.

ACT

In football, audibles allow quarterbacks to adjust the play based on what they think will work best. Write down some audibles for your life. How can you do the things you did at first in the life situation that you currently find yourself in?

Web Link
Did you know that you can be a missionary right now?

Snap the QR code with your smartphone or visit www.landofenough.com

DAY 21:
UNFINISHED

What do you still have left to do?

Are you believing your own hype?

SCRIPTURE

Revelation 3:1-6
Revelation 3:14-22
Hebrews 12:12-13

MISSION CHALLENGE

The Goliath: Share your faith with an intimidating person that you have avoided. Pray for confidence and impact from your great and powerful God.

WE'RE NOT DONE YET

As we spend another day with the churches in Revelation we see dire situations in Sardis and Laodicea. The church in Sardis is dying. The church in Laodicea is giving Jesus indigestion. Worst of all, both churches think they are doing fine. Such is the deadly self-deception of materialism! The Christians of Sardis took comfort in their reputation. The Christians of Laodicea took comfort in their wealth. As churches and individuals we face these potential pitfalls today.

Jesus reminds them that he has found their deeds unfinished in his sight. We would do well to remember this. Being a disciple of Jesus isn't about having a few good years. Being a disciple of Jesus means you aren't done until you're dead. We can't believe our own press and look at the churches we've built and the variety of ministries that we have and think we've done it. Instead, we should look at the lost all around us and think we've got so much more to do.

Here's where the lessons from the last few weeks and this week's lessons on mission intersect. Comfort kills our sharing. Whether it's sharing our wealth or sharing our faith, comfort blinds us to the needs all around us and eventually it even takes away our need for God. Being comfortable itself is not a sin. But trusting in that comfort is what kills our spirits because we stop trusting in God. If we've been trusting in comfort, Jesus would counsel us to repent and get strong by relying on the only one who is truly strong.

We may feel safe now, as the disciples in Ukraine did, but overnight everything can change. It's then that the true source of our strength will be revealed. May we be strong in the Lord!

REFLECT AND WRITE

If Jesus looked at your life like one of the churches in Revelation what would he say? Are there any areas where your reputation doesn't match what's really going on when no one sees you?

When it comes to making disciples there is much unfinished in all of our communities. Who do you still need to share your faith with? Is there a family member who doesn't really know that you are a disciple? Do the people at work know how much you love Jesus? Are your kids seeing the same devotion from you at home as they see from you at church?

ACT

Get your calculator out! Let's do some mission math. Record the number of members in your church. Now divide that number by the number of people in your metro area. That is the percentage of the mission that is complete in your town. How does that make you feel?

Now take the number of people in your town and divide it by 100. That is the number of disciples you would need in your town to have just 1% saved. It's time to get to work!

> **Web Link**
> Share your missions math on our Facebook page.
>
> Snap the QR code with your smartphone or visit www.landofenough.com

EXCUSES

If you took away all excuses what kind of impact could you have?

SCRIPTURE

Luke 14:15-24
Judges 3:31
1 Corinthians 9:22

MISSION CHALLENGE

The Paul: Share your faith with someone by being interested in something they like. Maybe you already share a hobby or an activity with someone. Let them know about your love for Christ.

JUST DO WHAT YOU CAN

What keeps us from being on the mission? We may feel like we don't have enough knowledge. We may have been rejected or even persecuted in the past. We may have just fallen out of the habit. Whatever the reason we need to overcome.

The parable of the great banquet casts our reasons in a different light. Life with Jesus is portrayed as an amazing party but instead of living the life and going to the banquet people have reasons, or as Luke puts it, excuses. We can't let excuses keep us from the great banquet and the great mission of Jesus. Our excuses not only keep us from pleasing God, they keep us from bringing others into God's glorious kingdom too.

In the book of Judges we find Shamgar. He only gets this one verse in the Bible, but even one verse in the Bible is remarkable. He's no Deborah or Samson yet he too saves Israel.

It takes a little imagination to understand how Shamgar could have killed 600 Philistines with an ox goad. After all, an ox goad is really just a pointy stick. Think about the excuses Shamgar could have made as Philistines came through his land and he had no sword or spear! But instead he did what he could, with what he had, where he was.

It is easy to marvel at the endurance of the disciples we've met from other countries in this passport. But we should also marvel at their mission focus. With less resources and less opportunity they do what they can, with what they have, where they are. Even in the turmoil of Ukraine great things are happening and souls are being saved because the disciples refuse to make excuses.

REFLECT AND WRITE

Let's think like Shamgar: What does God want you to do? How many would he have you impact and save? How should you do it? Host a Bible talk? Start a ministry?

Where would God want you to be on his mission? Maybe you are being called to go on a mission team or to help in a foreign country. Don't make excuses! However, it is more likely that God wants you to save many right where you are.

What resources do you have that can help people be saved? Are you ready to study the Bible with people? Do you have invitations? Do you have relationships outside of church? Be like Shamgar and Paul and do whatever it takes to save some.

ACT

Start something new. A new Bible study, a new Bible talk, a new outreach event or a new ministry can breath life into a whole church. Talk to your ministry leader about what your church needs and what you can do. Get other people to join you in your new thing and see how mighty God is to save!

Web Link
It's time to stock up on evangelism resources. Be prepared!

Snap the QR code with your smartphone or visit www.landofenough.com

DAY 23:
RELIANCE

Does the radical nature of your life force you to rely on God?

SCRIPTURE

Philippians 1:21-26
2 Cor. 11:16-12:10
2 Cor. 5:14-17

MISSION CHALLENGE

The Barnabas: Take someone with you and share your faith. Pick a brother or sister or even one of your children to be your missionary partner.

TO LIVE IS CHRIST

Here's a tough question: Do you lack reliance on God because you have not put yourself out there to the point that you need to rely on him? If your times with God are flat and your prayers are not loud cries and tears, could it be that you don't have anything to cry out about? Is a missing mission keeping you from the necessity of total reliance on God?

By all accounts Paul lived a wild life. His life was filled with high highs and low lows (like spending a night and a day in the open sea). When we signed up as followers of Christ we signed up for adventure. While we may never come close to the danger and excitement of Paul's missions, "regular" should not be a word that describes a Christ-focused life. We can go weeks, months and even years having average devotional times and being "okay." We think that if we could draw nearer to God in the word or through prayer that we could come out of our rut and be on fire for God. But maybe the opposite is true. Maybe the reason our times in the Bible and our prayers are only okay is because we aren't challenging ourselves with the mission to the point that we really need to rely on God.

What if you really put yourself out there? What if you determined that you were going to go and make a disciple? How much would you need to rely on God to see that happen? How would your Bible study and prayer change?

REFLECT AND WRITE

What would it take for you to make another disciple of Jesus Christ?

We spent time making budgets for our money and time. Now let's calculate the commitment and change we need to make in order to change someone's eternal destiny.

Write what needs to change in each of these "mission budget" categories: Personal Bible study, prayer, evangelism, church commitment, hospitality, follow-up and one-on-one Bible studies.

ACT

Put your new "mission budget" into action. Read and pray like someone on a mission for God because you are! When there is a setback or the mission gets tough remember to rely on God. That's what it's all about. Share your mission budget with your small group or accountability partner.

Web Link
Being a disciple is supposed to be an adventure.

Snap the QR code with your smartphone or visit www.landofenough.com

DAY 24:
HOPE

Are you involved in the mission of helping the hurting?

SCRIPTURE

Luke 4:16-21
James 1:27

MISSION CHALLENGE

The Bartimaeus: Share your faith and more with someone who is in need. You could give food to a home-less person or help an elderly person with groceries. Be sure to also tell them about Jesus and invite them to church or to your home.

THE MISSION OF HOPE

While Jesus' ultimate mission was to seek and save the lost, he also met people where they were. A lot of the people Jesus interacted with needed more than spiritual healing. Jesus used physical healing to show God's glory to the world. This book has focused on giving to missions and helping churches in the third world. If you give to support ministries and staff in the third world you are truly using your money to make a great impact. Missions funds may not directly help the poor and needy but they ultimately help them by giving purpose, healing and direction.

Our family of churches is blessed to be connected with one the world's top charities: HOPE *worldwide*. (See today's web link for more information.) HOPE *worldwide* works with the third world churches that we support to meet the physical, educational and emotional needs of the hurting. Many of our churches also have local chapters that help the hurting in our own towns. Make today the day that you donate or participate in a HOPE *worldwide* project!

Serving the needy abroad and in our communities is a great blessing. But we don't necessarily need organizations like HOPE *worldwide* to have impact. There are hurting and needy people in the seats next to us at every church service. There are hurting kids. There are lonely disciples. Our hearts, even more than our great organizational ties, will ultimately determine the impact we have on the hurting and needy in the world.

REFLECT AND WRITE

Is your heart for the poor and hurting in the right place? Do you look around at the relationships in your life with a desire to meet needs or do you look down on people who are in need?

Write a list of people that you know who may need encouragement. What could you do to encourage each person?

ACT

Follow today's web link and check out what HOPE *worldwide* is doing. Pray for them to have great impact. Sign up to be an annual giver and look at what other programs you or your family could participate in like Youth Corps or Volunteer Corps. Join the mission of HOPE *worlwide* today!

REST AND REFLECT

USE THIS SPACE TO REVIEW
THIS WEEK'S LESSONS AND
TAKE NOTES ON SUNDAY'S
SERMON.

_____
_____
_____
_____
_____
_____
_____
_____
_____
_____
_____
_____
_____
_____
_____
_____
_____
_____
_____
_____
_____
_____
_____
_____
_____
_____

WEEK FIVE

CELEBRATION

CELEBRATION

"Come with me and see my zeal for the Lord."

—2 Kings 10:16

We have a chance to inspire and make multigenerational change based on how we respond to God's word for rich Christians. We have a chance to change the first world and the third world by the power of God. As we come to the end of our journey to the "Land of Enough," ask yourself if you want to be an inspiration to your spouse, your children, your church and the poor. You can inspire!

In 2 Kings 10, Jehu goes on a God-inspired rampage against the evil in Israel. He was a famously reckless chariot driver. He pulls over in the middle of his coup and asks a man named Jehonadab if he wants a ride saying, "Come with me and see my zeal for the Lord!" Jehonadab climbs aboard. We don't immediately see the effect of Jehu's zeal on Jehonadab. That's how it often is when we make radical decisions. Maybe you are still waiting to see a difference from the changes you've made this month. Eventually, we do see the impact of Jehu's zeal. But we have to travel some 130 years and to the book of Jeremiah, chapter 35. There, Jeremiah honors the Rechabites as heroes of the time. The Rechabites took a vow a few generations earlier that said they would not drink wine, build houses or sow seeds. They would live in tents (intense!) and be simple, "enough is enough" kinds of people. Who were the Rechabites? They were the descendants of Jehonadab. It's cool to imagine that the ride with Jehu had hundreds of years of effect. We can have that same effect if we are willing to show our zeal for the Lord! What will your zeal accomplish in your children? How will the changes you've made this month impact children you may never meet who will receive your wealth as you gear your life toward giving?

Let's dream. Let's celebrate. Let's be modern-day heroes!

This week we'll celebrate the changes we've made and inspire one another as we continue our journey with God carrying new convictions about wealth and mission!

IF YOU LIVED IN LATIN AMERICA OR THE CARIBBEAN...

Celebration and joy are hallmarks of Latin and Caribbean culture. If you've ever been to one of these churches then you know that the spirit of Christ only increases the joy of our brothers and sisters. That joy bubbles over in their lives despite the extreme financial hardship that many disciples face. Opportunities for success are hard to come by in countries that have low educational standards and corrupt governments. But what the Christians in these countries have to offer is priceless: an opportunity to find salvation through the message of Jesus Christ.

It may be hard to imagine, but our change of heart toward wealth and mission has the potential to change many lives in these countries. People with sacrificial hearts who came from the first world to the third world began these churches. Those same sacrificial hearts will keep these churches growing and multiplying.

In our final week we will look at heroes from the first world and dream about becoming heroes ourselves. One such set of heroes is Wilner and Chantel Cornely. They have led churches in Haiti, the Midwest and anywhere that God called them (like Boston, Miami, New York, Johannesburg, Madagascar, Mauritius, Phoenix, Chicago and Detroit!). After living in Chicago and Detroit they were called back to lead the churches in Jamaica. They left family and friends behind to serve with joy. Unfortunately, shortly after arriving in Kingston, Wilner was diagnosed with cancer. Thus far, God has allowed him to outlive his doctor's expectations and spend quality time impacting his family and the church. They are a heroic example of living the mission!

In all of our churches there are heroes. There are giving heroes, serving heroes and evangelizing heroes. The question we should ask ourselves as we go through this last week of devotionals is, "How can I be a hero for God?" If we focus on others instead of ourselves by limiting the money, time and stuff that we require then we truly have reason to celebrate. You may never lead a church as a missionary and the churches we support may never know your name, but they will know that they have a hero whom God used to bring them salvation because of the lasting changes that you've made this month.

MISSION CHALLENGES

The focus of our last week of mission challenges is making a difference. By giving sacrificially to world missions or charity we go beyond experiencing life in the third world and actually change the world, even if our contribution seems small. Plan, give and encourage others to give. May all of your experiences this month add up and overflow into a joyful offering.

Day 25
Choose your own adventure! Can you think of a creative way to sacrifice and save? Go for it! Share your idea on our Facebook page.

Day 26
Give and give some more. Examine what you've given or planned to give for special missions contribution or your charity. Decide to give even more. Every little bit of extra adds up to an amazing gift.

Day 27
Prayer is powerful. Pray for everyone in your small group to cheerfully and sacrificially give. Pray for them to have lasting change from the lessons learned this month.

Day 28
Go on a prayer walk in a cemetery. Pray about the impact you are having with your life. Pray to be dead to the things of this world. Thank God for making you truly alive.

Day 29
Write an encouraging card to a brother or sister. Has someone had a hard time this month? Has someone inspired you by their example? Let them know with a loving card.

Day 30
Set up a savings plan for next year's special missions contribution or a charity. Use a piggy bank or an old coffee can as a place to store your change. Don't dip into it until it's time to give next year!

FAMILY NIGHT DEVOTIONAL

Sing

Scripture Acts 3:19

Discuss Recap the lessons you've learned this month. Talk about how you gave to world missions or charity and how that money will help God's kingdom. Ask the question: What does it mean to be refreshed?

Activity Have a refreshment challenge. Pour a big glass of icy lemonade or soda and make a bowl of ice cream. Have each person in your family taste test and decide which is more refreshing on a hot day. Talk about the results of your family survey.

Game In celebration of a sacrificial month, have a dance party. To make it into a game you can judge each other. The winner is the one whose dancing is the most refreshing!

Pray!

RECIPE OF THE WEEK

Beyen are delicious fried bananas from Haiti. This is an Americanized recipe that is low in cost and high in deliciousness. This is definitely a recipe that the kids can help with. What a great way to celebrate!

Ingredients
2-6 Bananas
Frying oil
Complete pancake and waffle mix
Sugar
Cinnamon
Honey (optional)
Ice cream (optional)

landofenough.com/recipes

DAY 25:
CHANGE

How have my heart and actions changed this month?

SCRIPTURE

2 Corinthians 7:10-11

Matthew 7:15-20

Acts 3:19

MISSION CHALLENGE

Choose your own adventure! Can you think of a creative way to sacrifice and save? Go for it! Share your idea on our Facebook page.

CELEBRATE LASTING CHANGE

It's one thing to decide to change; it's another thing to make the changes last. On a churchwide level, we should welcome conversations about wealth in biblical terms more often. We may need to change the culture of our church from one that rarely and timidly speaks of wealth to one that boldly and frequently stands on the Scriptures' clear teachings about wealth. We need to become a herd of sheep and leave our "goat-ish" ways behind us for good. Furthermore, we cannot accept a lack of mission in our lives or our churches.

Lasting change is difficult. Look at the decisions that you've made; how can you make them last? How has your discipleship partner or small group helped? Can you add wealth discussions to your discipleship times? What other ways can you make sure this continues to be an area of growth?

Repentance is often seen as a negative thing but it is actually a reason to celebrate! God has granted us an opportunity to change our hearts toward wealth and make a huge impact with our lives.

Some of these things are bigger decisions than we can make in one month. We should celebrate even

the smallest changes of attitude and heart because our society's thorny grip is very difficult to loosen.

Heroes: If you have made it this far on this journey to the Land of Enough you are a hero!

REFLECT AND WRITE

Have you made and stuck to a budget?

Are you scheduling your time for impact?

Have you set spiritual goals for your life and your family?

Are you meeting with your spouse/ roommates weekly to plan ahead?

Have you given joyfully to special missions contribution at your local church or a reputable charity? Have you begun to tithe?

Have you set a wealth boundary? Have you set time boundaries?

Have you started to organize and simplify your possessions?

Are you on the mission field yourself?

What decisions would you still like to make? How could you go about making them soon?

ACT

We have so much to celebrate! God loves a cheerful giver and when we give in the ways we've learned about this month we can truly do it with great cheer. Find an inexpensive way to celebrate your accomplishments.

Web Link
See how your changes compare with others reading this book.

Snap the QR code with your smartphone or visit www.landofenough.com

SPECIAL

Have you sacrificially given to overseas missions this year?

SCRIPTURE

Isaiah 41:1-20

SPECIAL MISSIONS CONTRIBUTION

Throughout this month, as we've focused on our hearts toward wealth, we've also focused on giving to special overseas missions that meet needs in our sister churches. It's one thing to pare down and live with enough. It's another thing to give generously to people who really need it. **Giving to world missions is the best way you can give your money!**

In today's passage we see God's heart for his people all over the world. God wants the distant coastlands to hear his word. He wants the poor and needy to be helped. Many of us cannot travel to the places we support, take up a "one-suitcase challenge," or plant a church. But we can support such efforts cheerfully as we sacrifice and give in our own way each year for special missions contribution.

Heroes: Tim and Wendy Sherrill are living "special missions lives." They have served in churches while working full-time jobs throughout their lives. But a few years ago they felt called to lead and support a church full time. Tim retired early and supplemented himself with his retirement fund so he could lead the Fort Wayne Church of Christ. His radical desire to serve God's kingdom has been a great blessing!

How many more "special missions lives" could impact the world for God if we took radical, faithful leaps like the Sherrills? How many of our small churches, even in the U.S., would benefit from mature brothers and sisters retiring to go into the full-time ministry?

REFLECT AND WRITE

Have you sacrificially given to world missions this year?

Do you understand where your church gives money and what it does? Understanding helps us feel connected with the people and churches that we support.

Looking ahead, can you think of anything that you could do to give even more next year?

How have these devotionals or the mission challenges helped you give more?

Are you going to adopt as a lifestyle any of the mission challenges you've done?

ACT

Give to special missions contribution or a charity of your choice with a cheerful heart. Start dreaming about giving more and more each year and impacting this lost world with the resources God is giving you.

Web Link
Take a tour of the churches we support around the world.

Snap the QR code with your smartphone or visit www.landofenough.com

DAY 27:
SERVE

How do you feel about being a servant?

SCRIPTURE

Ephesians 5:15-33

MISSION CHALLENGE

Prayer is powerful. Pray for everyone in your small group to cheerfully and sacrificially give. Pray for them to have lasting change from the lessons learned this month.

TIME TO SERVE WITHOUT STRESS

For some of us, writing a check is difficult. For others, giving up time may be much harder than giving money. Today we will focus on giving our time and our very selves to the mission with happy hearts.

Earlier, we learned about the importance of scheduling for success. Burnout often happens when we give a lot of our time to ministry but are not disciplined. We start to blame church, church people and even God for our hectic schedules even though it's ultimately on us. Yes, we need to sacrificially serve God with our time, but we cannot serve the church at the expense of our family. Burnout can be avoided! We should look no further than the example of Jesus himself who often sought time away with his disciples to be refreshed.

It is interesting that Paul writes about being careful with our time right before the most extensive teaching on marriage and parenting in the Bible. "Making the most of every opportunity" literally means redeeming the time or buying it back. For those of us who want to have solid walks with God and raise our families in the Lord, we must take this advice to heart! Build a great foundation by scheduling for success!

Heroes: Every year after graduation from college, some of our students take one year challenges locally and abroad. They sacrifice time and money to serve in the ministry, often putting their careers on hold. Our special missions contribution helps fund their radical acts of service!

REFLECT AND WRITE

Have you started having a weekly meeting with your spouse or roommates?

How was it? What could be done to improve it? How will you keep it going?

Did it set you up for success in spirituality, parenting and finances?

Celebrate the victory and don't let the good habit fall by the wayside!

ACT

Get your calendar out and schedule dates and times that you will serve. Plan a few months in advance so that serving will always be something you look forward to and not a last-minute burden.

Web Link
Still not sure how you can help? Over 50 serving ideas.

Snap the QR code with your smartphone or visit www.landofenough.com

DAY 28:
EXAMPLE

How does your lifestyle preach to your family and friends?

SCRIPTURE

Romans 12:1-2

MISSION CHALLENGE

Go on a prayer walk in a cemetery. Pray about the impact you are having with your life. Pray to be dead to the things of this world. Thank God for making you truly alive.

COUNTER CULTURAL ENCOUNTERS

As we continue with our celebration week, consider the impact a mission-focused life with wealth, time and possession boundaries can have. Taking a stand in these areas is radical in our society that is sure to draw attention. Many people may not understand why you live differently. Others will be intrigued and possibly even spurred on toward a relationship with Christ. It is a constant battle to resist conforming to this age. If we can win the battle, the reward in this life and the next is awesome!

In his book, *Radical*, David Platt describes something that some families in his church were able to do after setting a wealth boundary. In their town there was a struggling neighborhood and school. A number of families decided to use their excess wealth to buy houses and move into the neighborhood and put their children in the struggling district. The neighborhood and school changed quickly due to their presence and influence. Has God put creative ideas like this on your heart?

Heroes: Ed Anton tells of a heroic example of nonconformity that brought him to Christ in his book, *Repentance.* He was a young rising star executive at Coca-Cola and had just bought a house in an upper-class neighborhood. He filled the house with furniture and filled the garage with a car. He had also moved in next to a family of disciples. When they invited him over he was shocked by what he didn't see. They were living well below their means. Their house looked empty. But they seemed so happy. This shock to his system helped open him up to studying the Bible and becoming a disciple.

REFLECT AND WRITE

Whether you've considered it or not, your example is having an impact. What does the example you set in the areas of wealth, time, stuff and mission tell the world about Jesus? Would anybody think that you are different or even weird, or do you nicely fit in with the world? What could you do differently that would get people thinking about your counter-cultural example?

ACT

Have a family meeting where you go through your house and talk about the example that you are setting with the things that you have.

Pray and dream about getting weird looks because your life is so different from the typical person in your social situation.

Web Link
Check out Ed Anton's book for yourself.

Snap the QR code with your smartphone or visit www.landofenough.com

DAY 29:
HOSPITALITY

Are you
practicing
kindness?

SCRIPTURE

Romans 12:13

MISSION CHALLENGE

Write an encouraging card to a brother or sister. Has someone had a hard time this month? Has someone inspired you by their example? Let them know with a loving card.

A CENTER FOR HOSPITALITY

Many of us have homes. What should we do with them? It is fatalism to think that we all need to move out and have no place to lay our head. It also can't be accepted that we just live in luxury while others suffer so much. There is a middle ground for those of us blessed enough to have housing. We should use what God has given us to be hospitable!

We can host church events, Bible studies, Bible talks, traveling disciples and much more with our homes, no matter what we think about how nice our homes are. Our cars should be available to those in need within reason. We should all carry open-fridge policies (you know you've got a friend when it's not weird to look in their fridge).

Hospitality and sharing with the saints is more than just a good idea: It is a command and even a requirement for someone who wants to be an elder in God's church.

One of the blessings of having our finances in order with wealth boundaries in place is that we can afford to spectacularly serve.

Dream about the impact that you can have with your house, your wealth and your stuff. Think about ways you can make your home a center of ministry and outreach to those in need of Jesus.

Heroes: In every church there are hospitality heroes. Whenever someone comes to town from another church they are quick to host and feed and serve. There is even a couple in Lansing , Michigan who finished their basement so they could be better hosts. They have a guest book filled with memories from the disciples they have hosted. Can you think of the hospitality heroes in your church?

REFLECT AND WRITE

What could you do to follow the Bible's commands about showing hospitality?

Are you guarded with your home and resources or do you cheerfully give?

Think about a time when someone really served you and showed true hospitality. How did it make you feel?

Is your home set up to be outward focused? What could you change to make your home a center for hospitality?

ACT

Have someone over with no agenda except to show them hospitality.

Decide to become a hospitality hero yourself.

Web Link
With these devotionals ending are you ready for what's next?

Snap the QR code with your smartphone or visit www.landofenough.com

DAY 30:
MORE

Are you ready to impact more by keeping less?

SCRIPTURE

1 Thessalonians 4:9-12

Colossians 3:22

2 Thessalonians 3:10-13

MISSION CHALLENGE

Set up a savings plan for next year's special missions contribution or a charity. Use a piggy bank or an old coffee can as a place to store your change. Don't dip into it until it's time to give next year!

MAKING, SAVING, AND GIVING MORE

Hopefully, as you've travelled through this passport, you've come closer than ever to the "Land of Enough."

Saying enough is enough does not mean that we live below our potential. We live below what we can afford. Very few of the people who read this should work less. There are some circumstances where people should pare down their workload to focus on people or things they've neglected. But most of us should do our best at work, which usually results in making more. However, when enough is enough, the more will go to those who really need it.

The Scriptures are clear when it comes to work ethic and idleness. So, let's work even harder since we are doing it for a higher purpose and with the goal of giving even more to those in need!

Heroes: We have a lot of work to do. The map of churches may look like we have it pretty well covered but there are many areas unreached. Planting a church requires funding and missionaries. If we can find both, missions will move from the pages of this book to the lost souls of the world.

Has God called you to the mission field? Instead of sacrificing to give to missions, you could be going on missions. In other words, you could be a hero.

REFLECT AND WRITE

Are you working and making enough to meet your needs and prepare for the future?

Would it help your relationship with God and with others to work less if possible?

Should you work more so that you could give more and help those who cannot help themselves?

What will it take to keep the convictions you've gained this month?

Now is the time to meet up with your accountability partner and discuss the changes you've made and get advice for your future.

ACT

Write down three things that you will change from the lessons you learned this month. Share them with someone who can help you to consistently put them into practice.

Web Link
Share your Passport experience with the world.

Snap the QR code with your smartphone or visit www.landofenough.com

REST AND REFLECT

USE THIS SPACE TO REVIEW
THIS WEEK'S LESSONS AND
TAKE NOTES ON SUNDAY'S
SERMON.

This book is dedicated to my
wife, Beth.

Joel Nagel has led the Lansing Area Church of Christ
in Lansing, Michigan since 2002. He studied history at Michigan State University where he focused on
building a campus ministry. When not advancing the
gospel or spending time with his family, Joel loves trail
running and exploring waterfalls in Michigan's Upper
Peninsula. He and his wife, Beth, have two daughters.

GOLDEN RULE

What God
Expects of
Every
Disciple

MEMBERSHIP

John Oakes with Ron and Linda Brumley

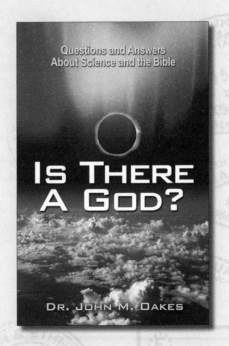

Questions and Answers
About Science and the Bible

IS THERE
A GOD?

DR. JOHN M. OAKES

Available at www.ipibooks.com

www.ipibooks.com